I0416626

This Book Belongs to

_____

_____

Copyright © 2024 by Jeny Alexa
All rights reserved.

No portion of this book may be reproduced in any form without the prior written permission from the publisher or author, except as permitted by U.S copyright law.

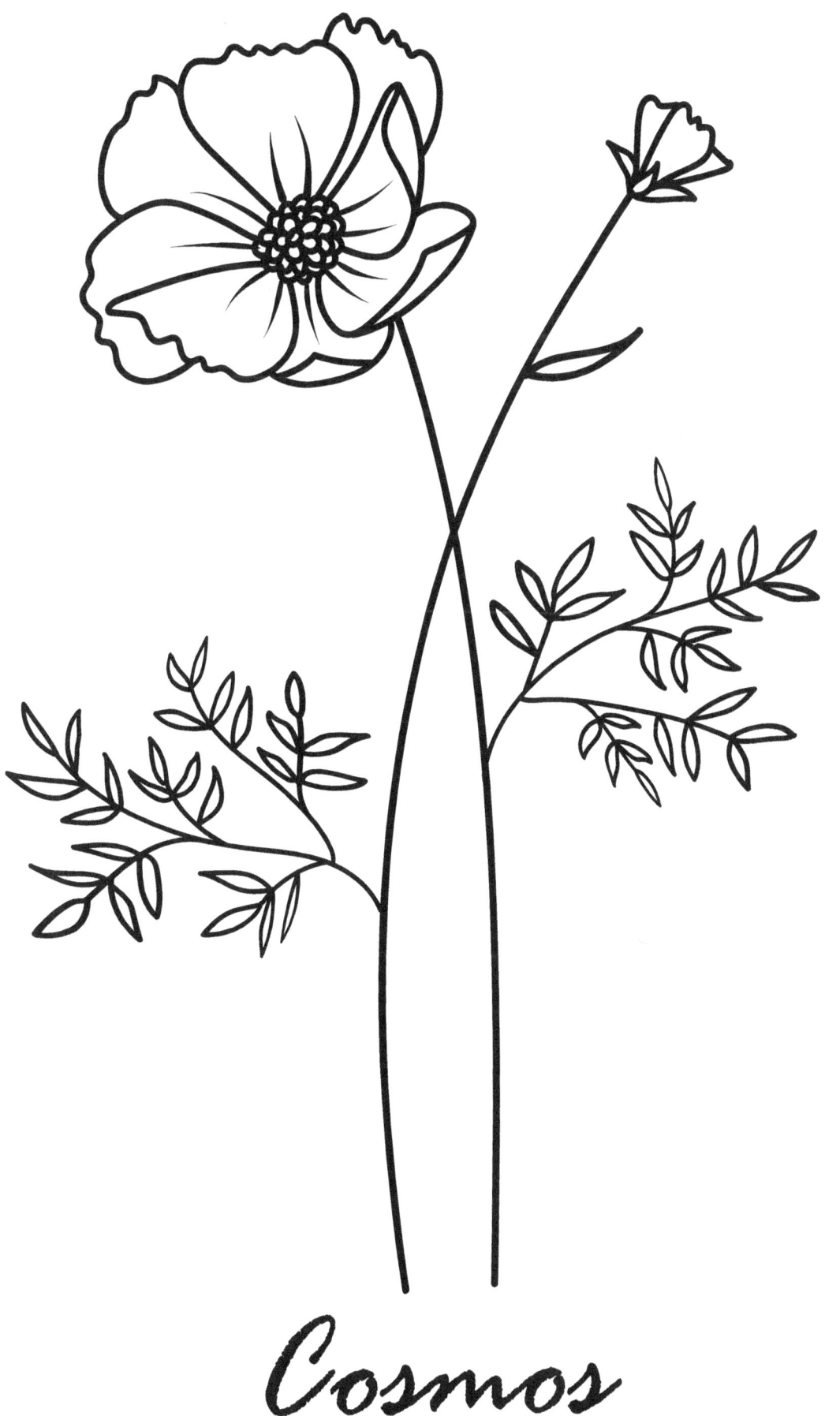

Cosmos

This Page is Intentionally Left Blank to Prevent Bleed Through.

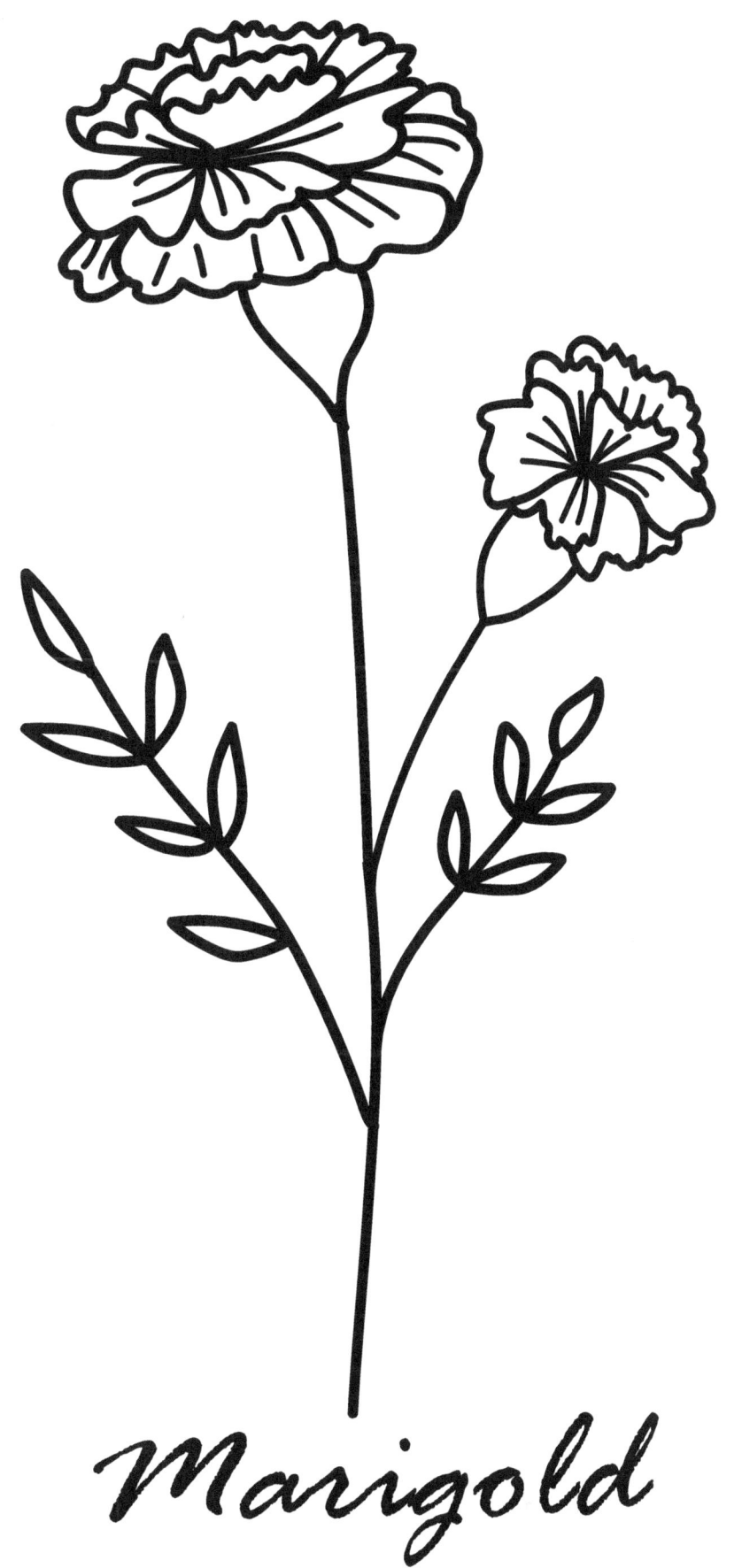

Marigold

This Page is Intentionally Left Blank to Prevent Bleed Through.

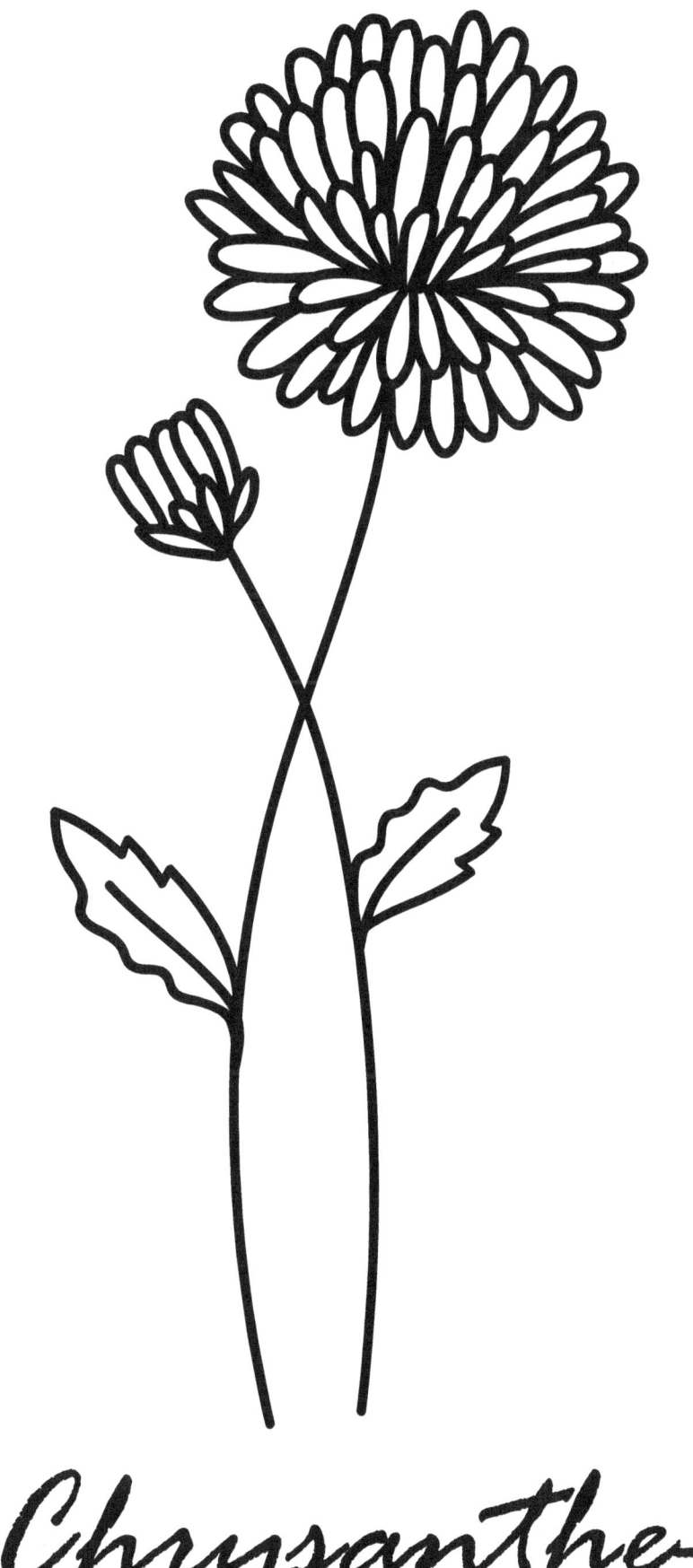

Chrysanthe-

This Page is Intentionally Left Blank to Prevent Bleed Through.

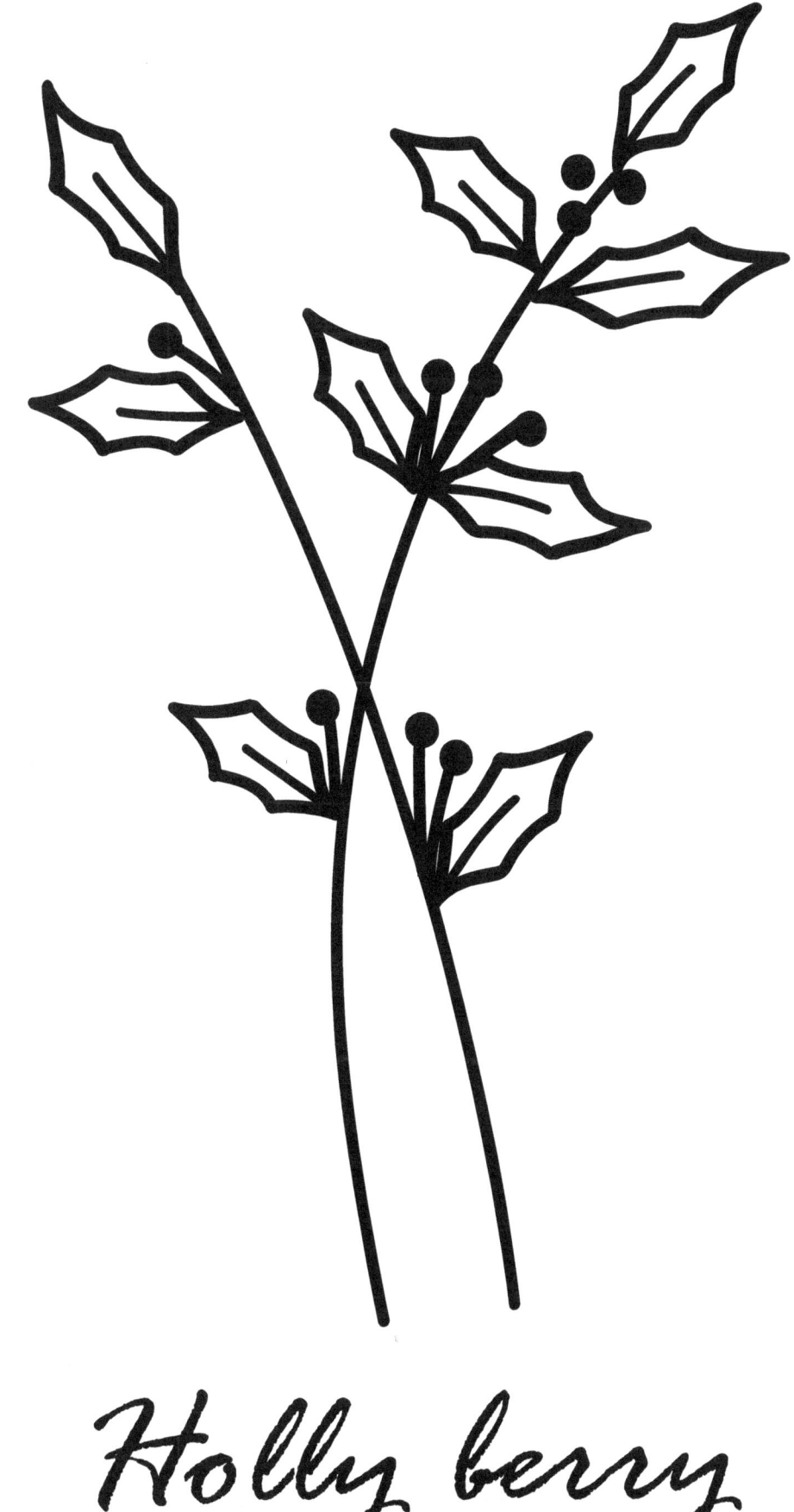

Holly berry

This Page is Intentionally Left Blank to Prevent Bleed Through.

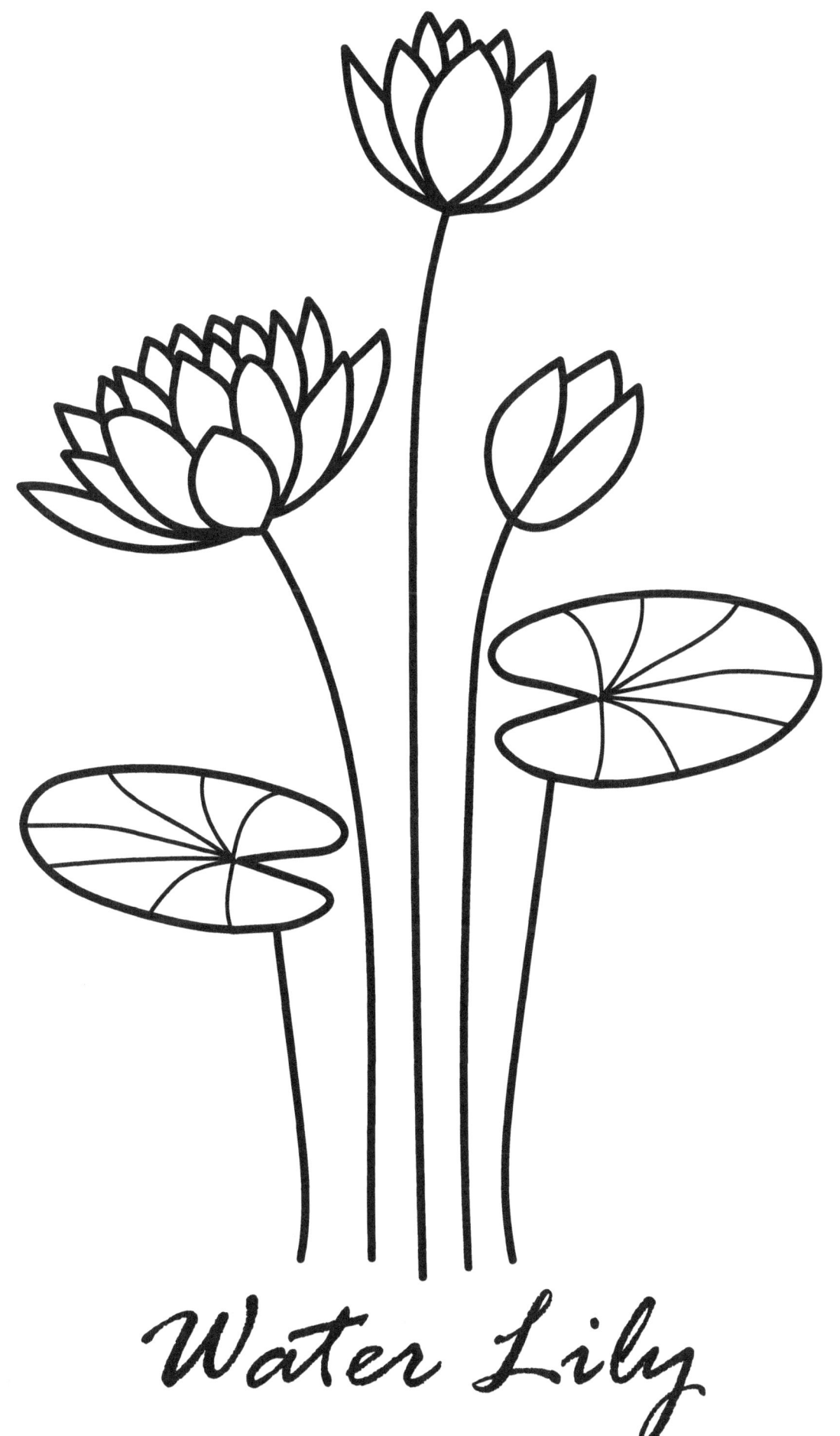

Water Lily

This Page is Intentionally Left Blank to Prevent Bleed Through.

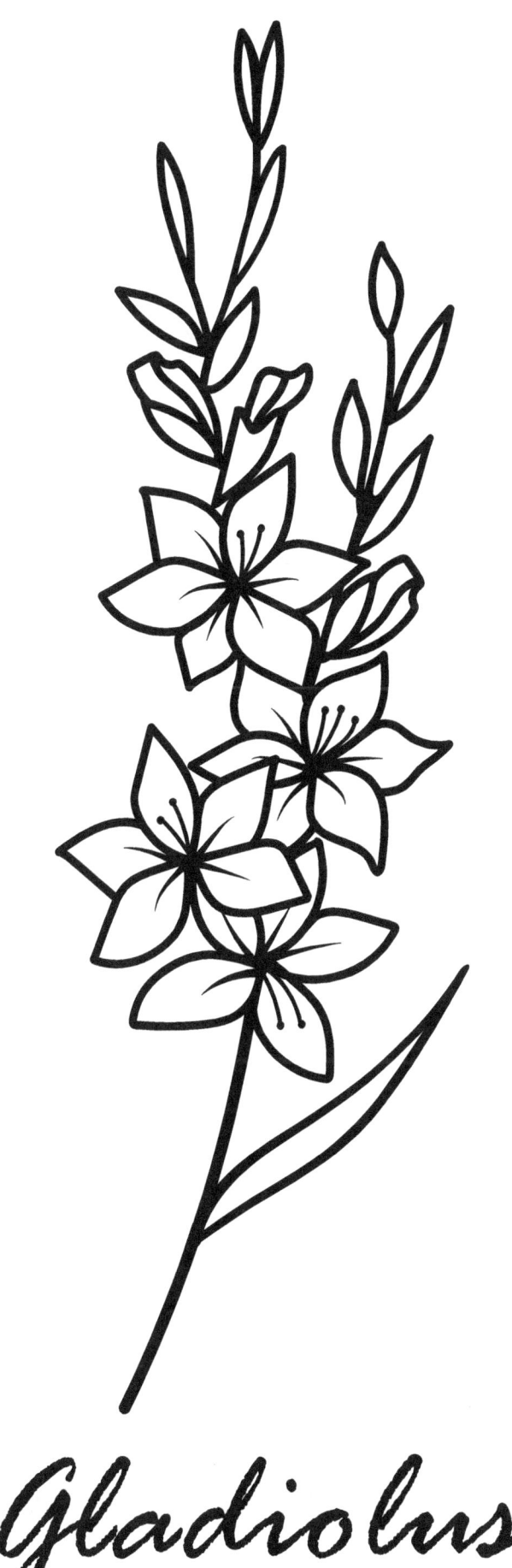

Gladiolus

This Page is Intentionally Left Blank to Prevent Bleed Through.

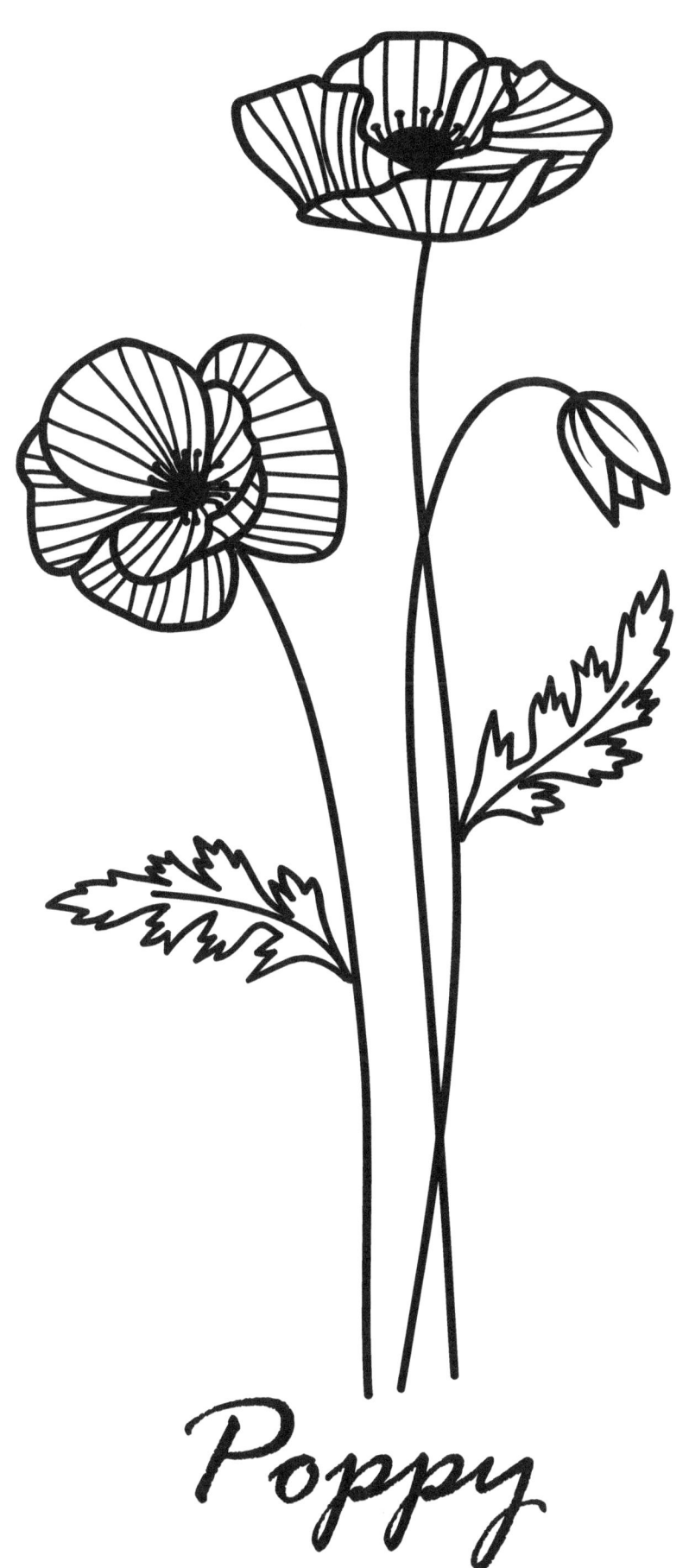

Poppy

This Page is Intentionally Left Blank to Prevent Bleed Through.

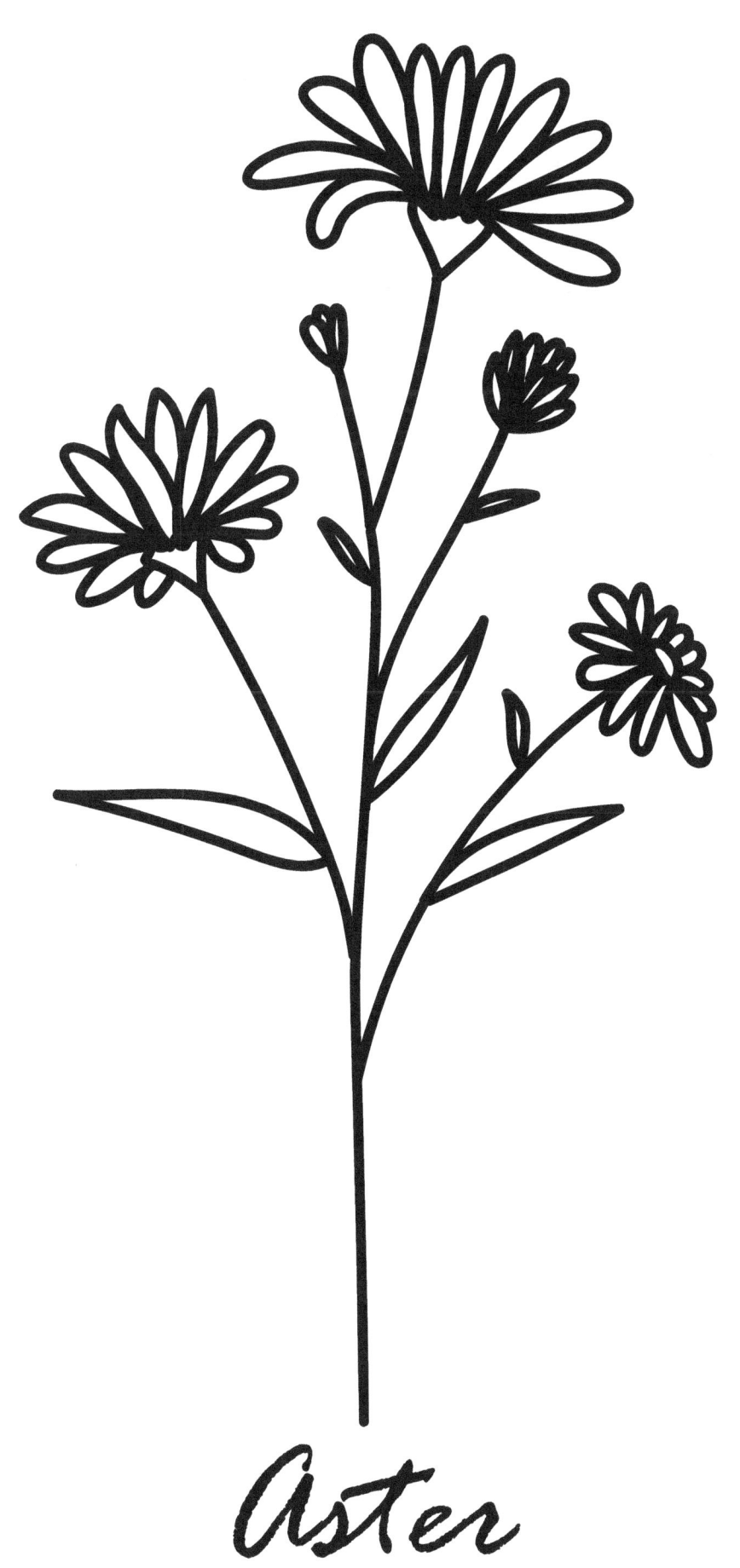

Aster

This Page is Intentionally Left Blank to Prevent Bleed Through.

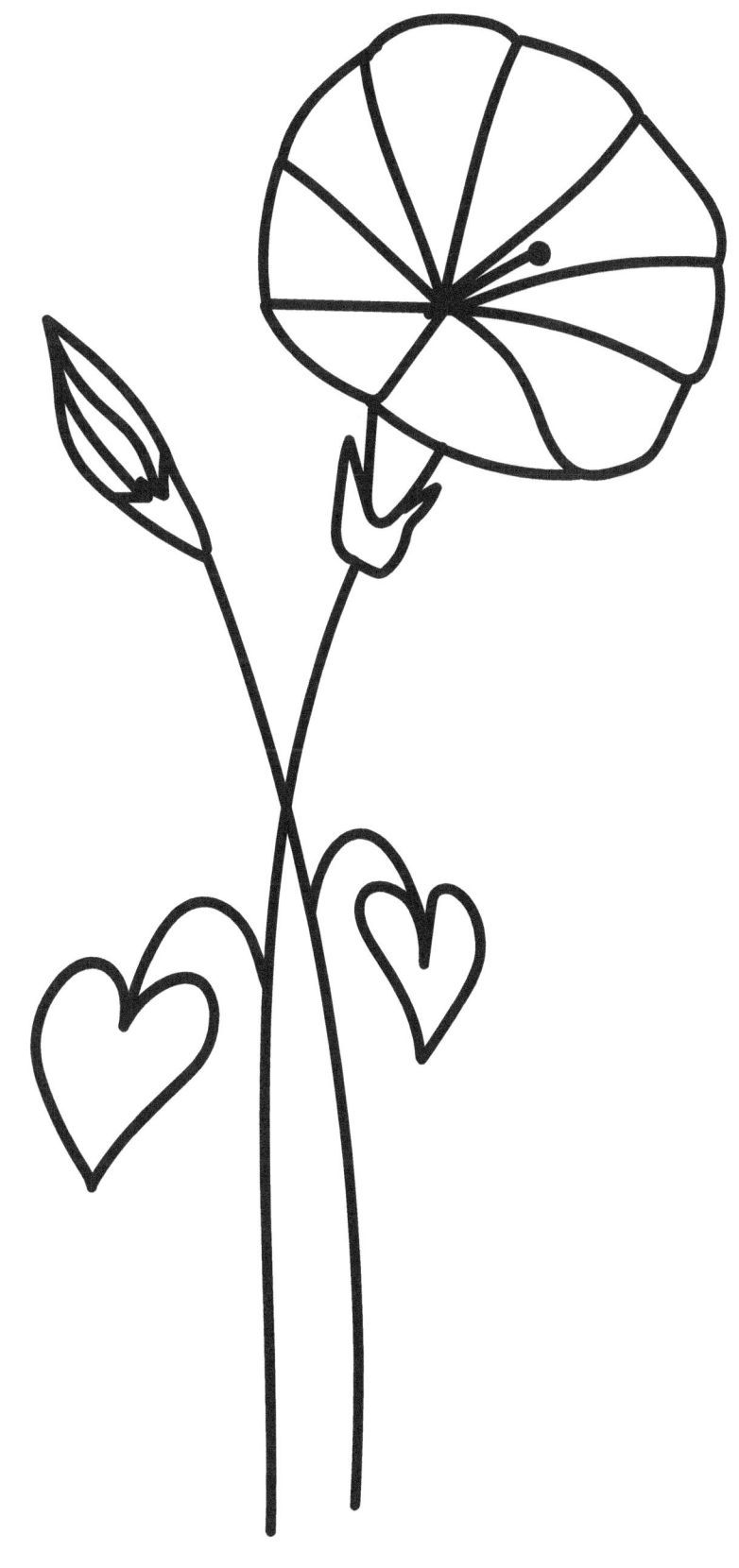

Morning Glory

This Page is Intentionally Left Blank to Prevent Bleed Through.

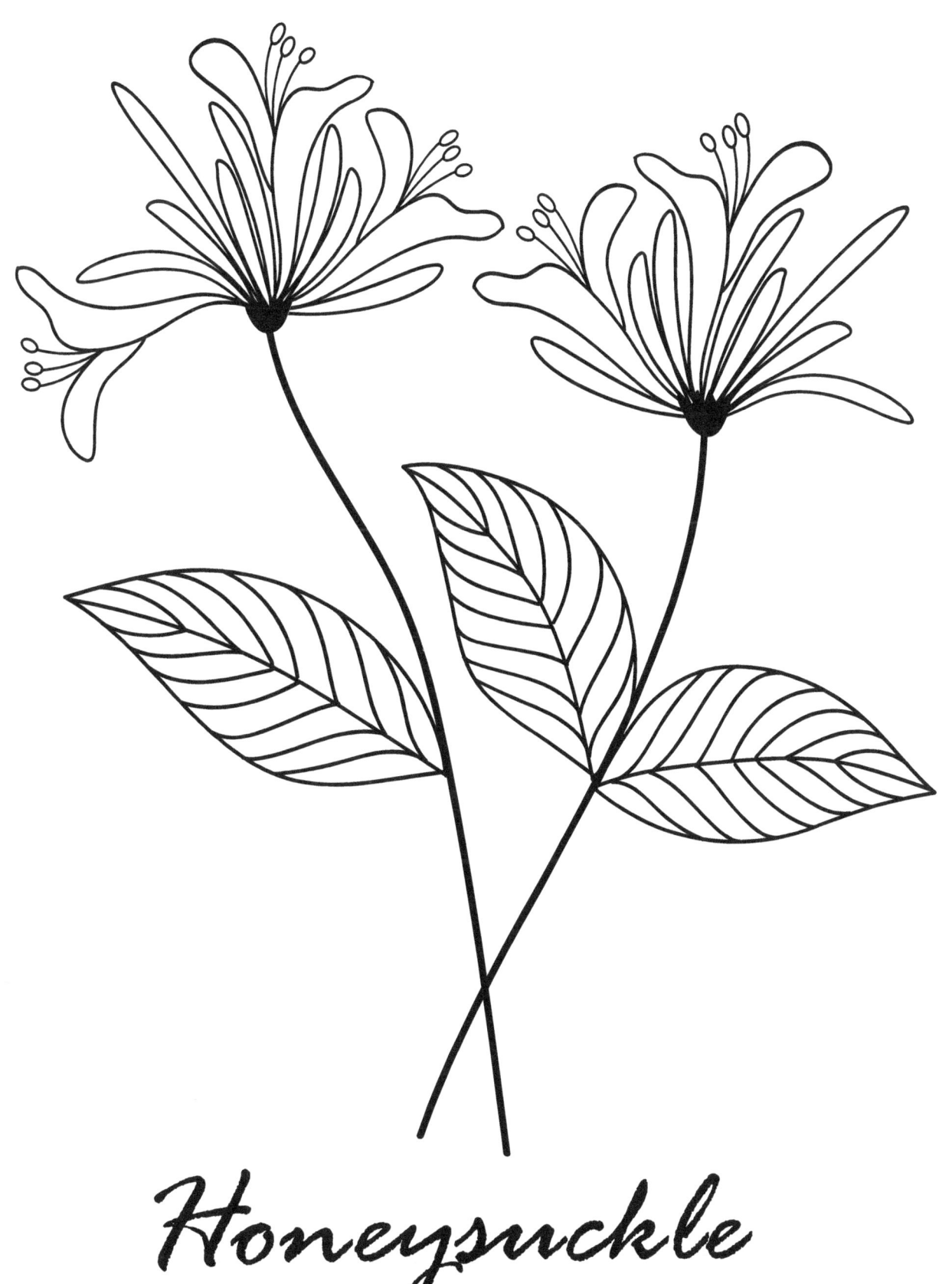

Honeysuckle

This Page is Intentionally Left Blank to Prevent Bleed Through.

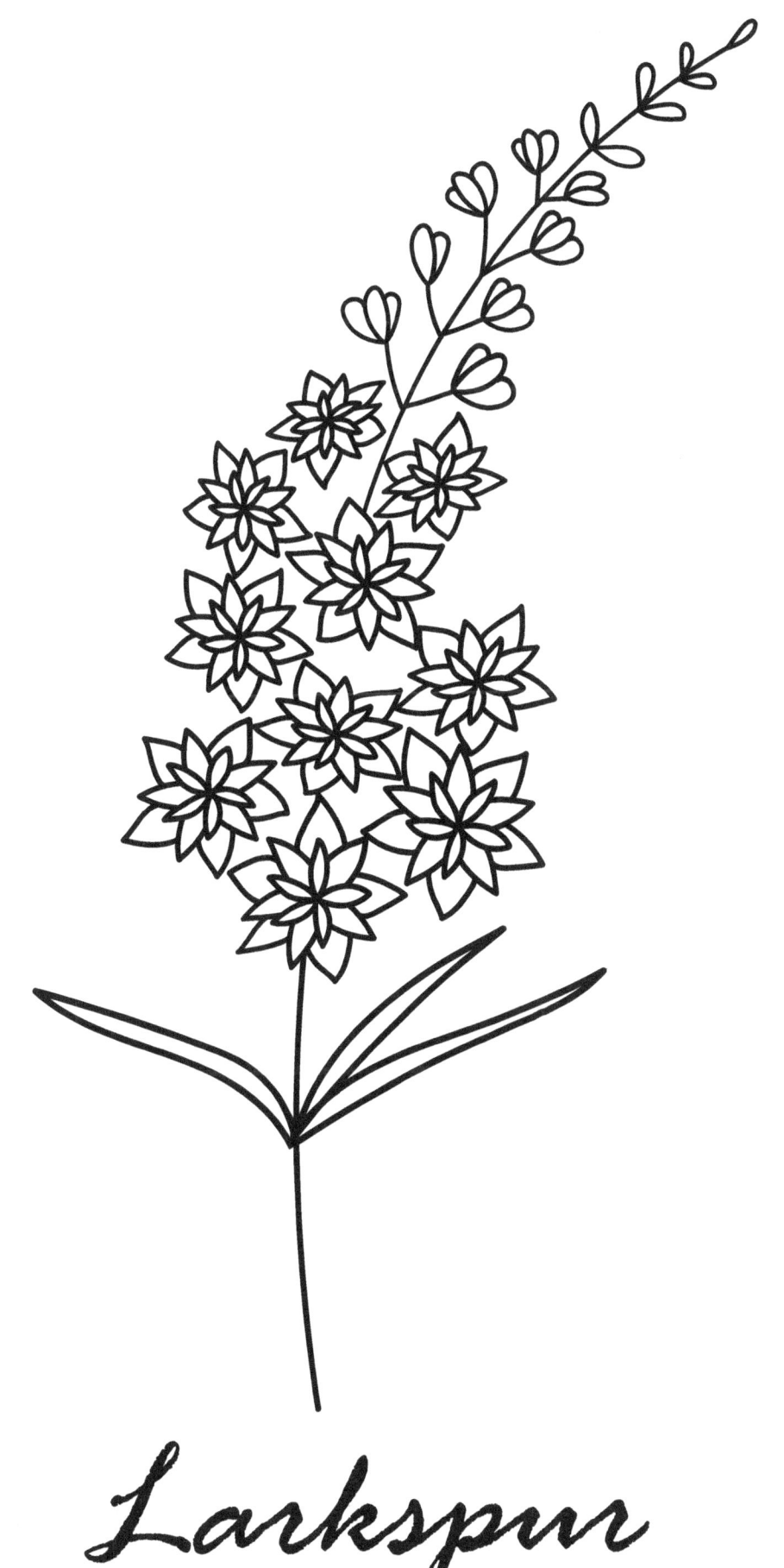

Larkspur

This Page is Intentionally Left Blank to Prevent Bleed Through.

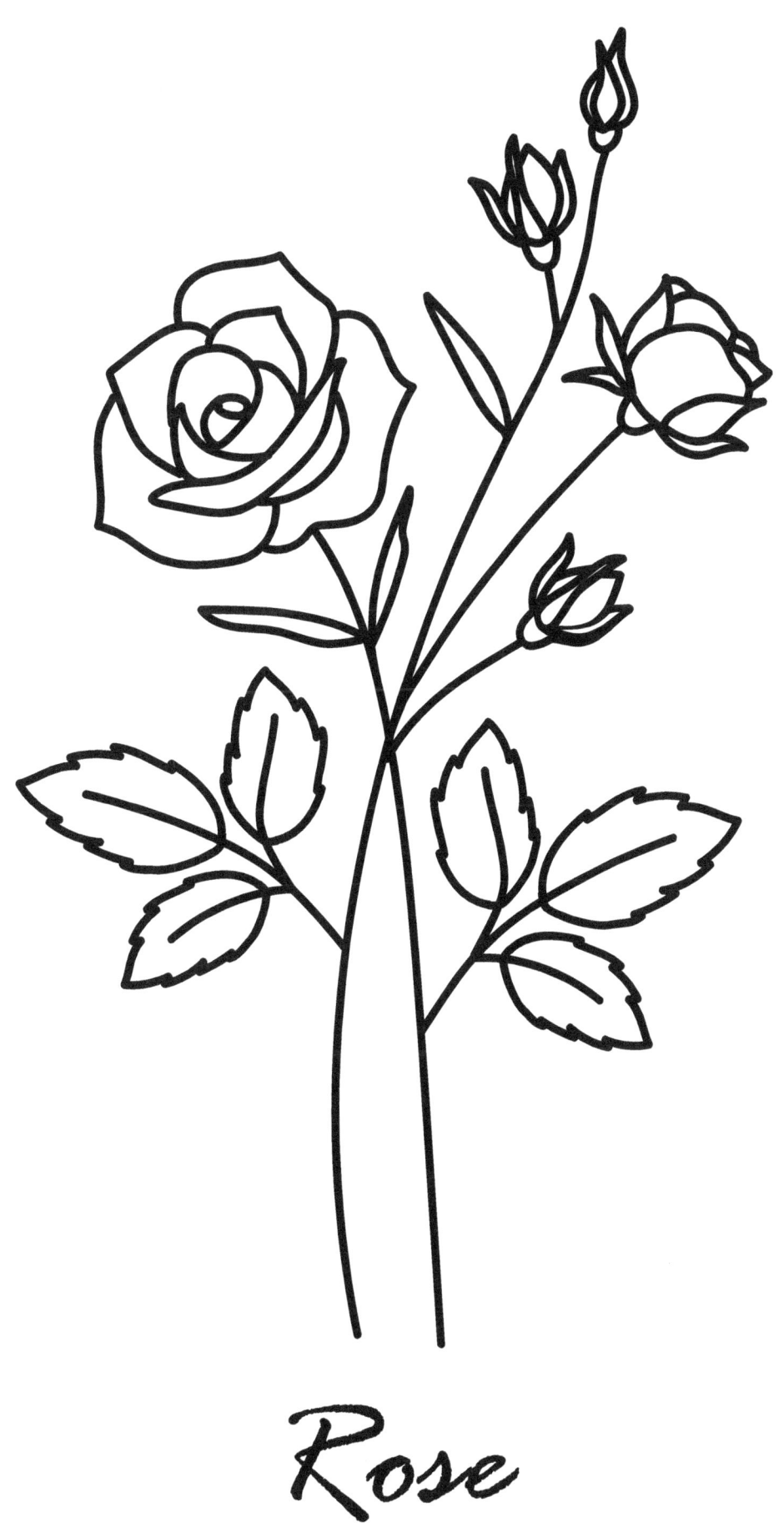

Rose

This Page is Intentionally Left Blank to Prevent Bleed Through.

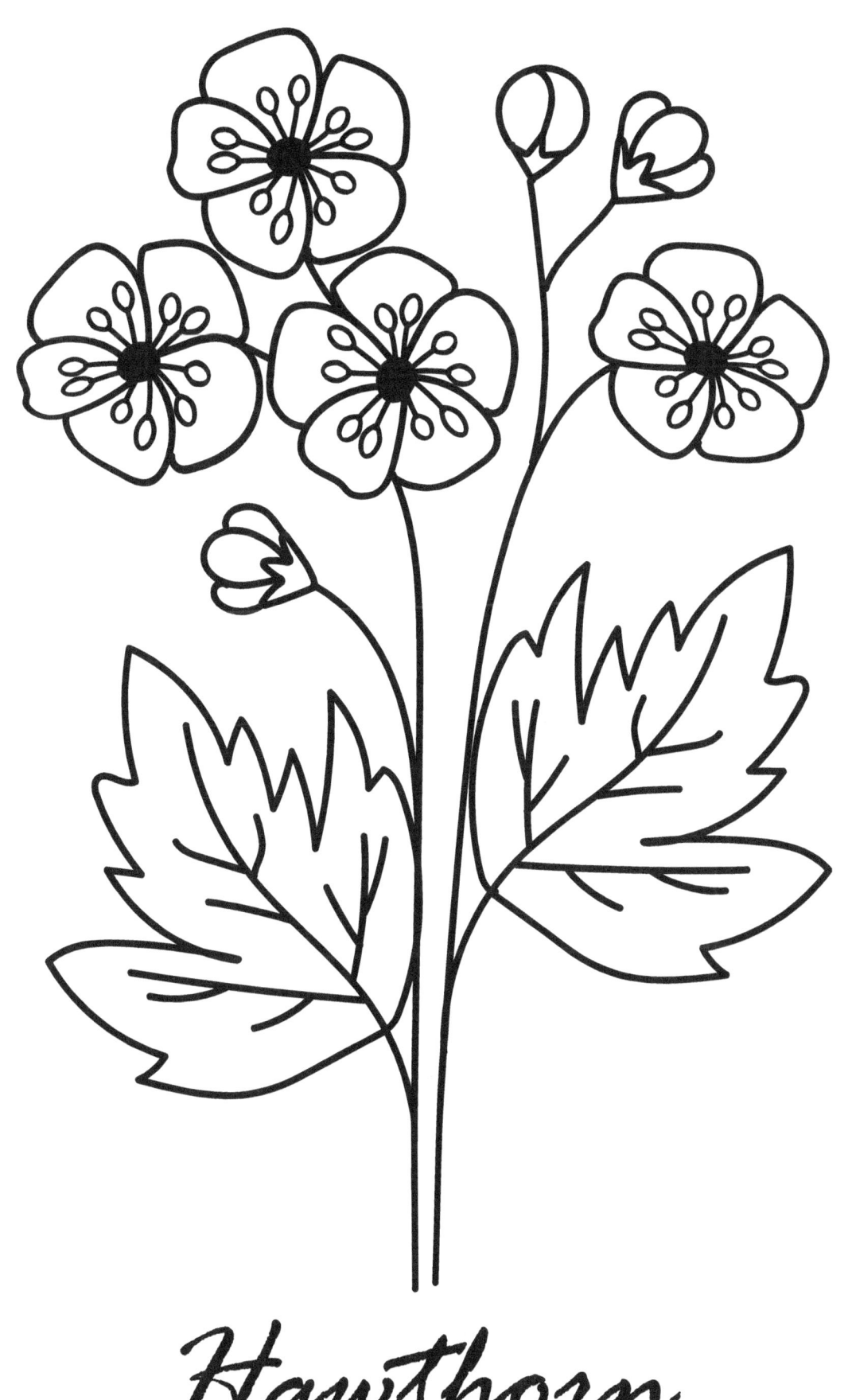

Hawthorn

This Page is Intentionally Left Blank to Prevent Bleed Through.

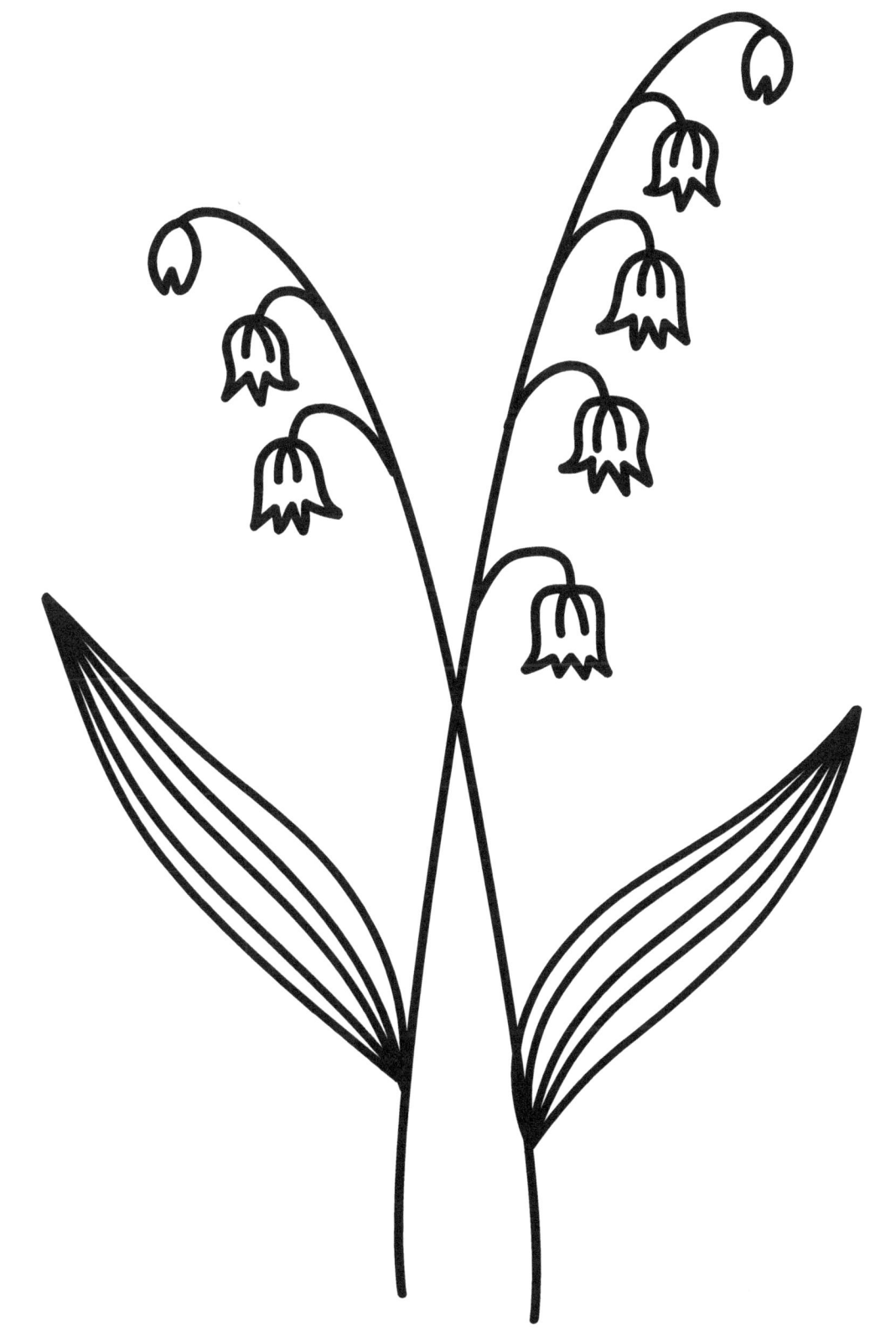

Lily of the Valley

This Page is Intentionally Left Blank to Prevent Bleed Through.

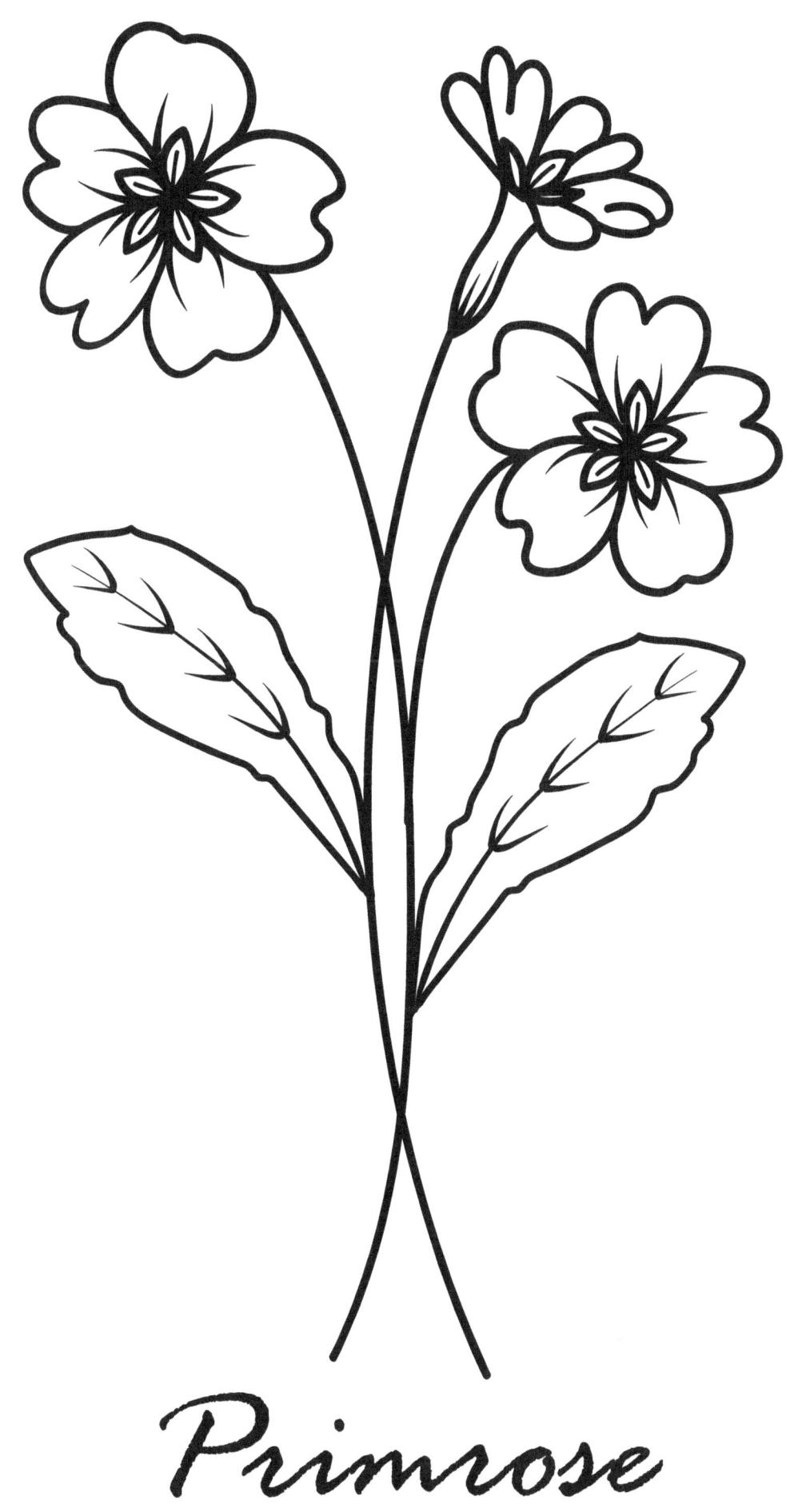

Primrose

This Page is Intentionally Left Blank to Prevent Bleed Through.

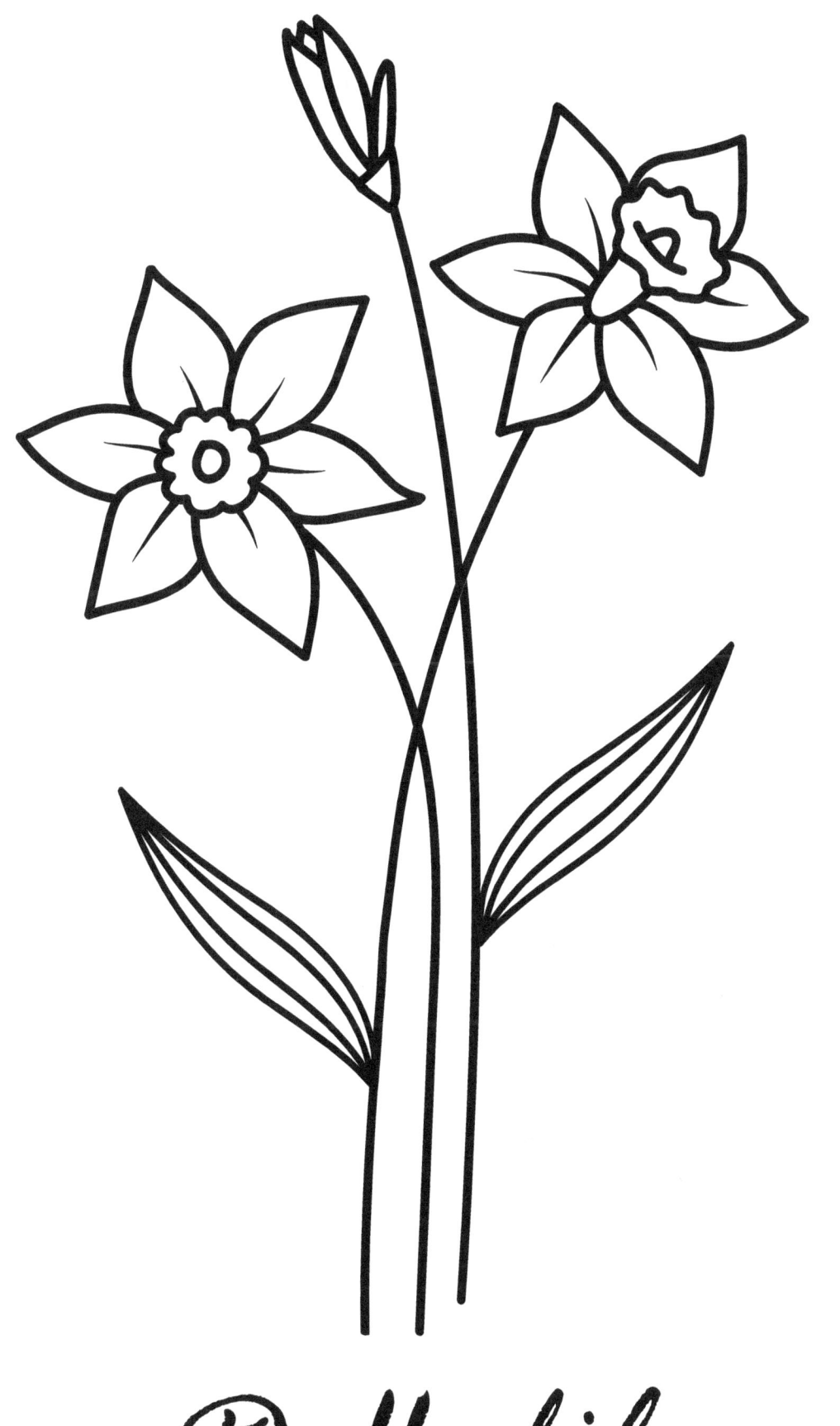

Daffodil

This Page is Intentionally Left Blank to Prevent Bleed Through.

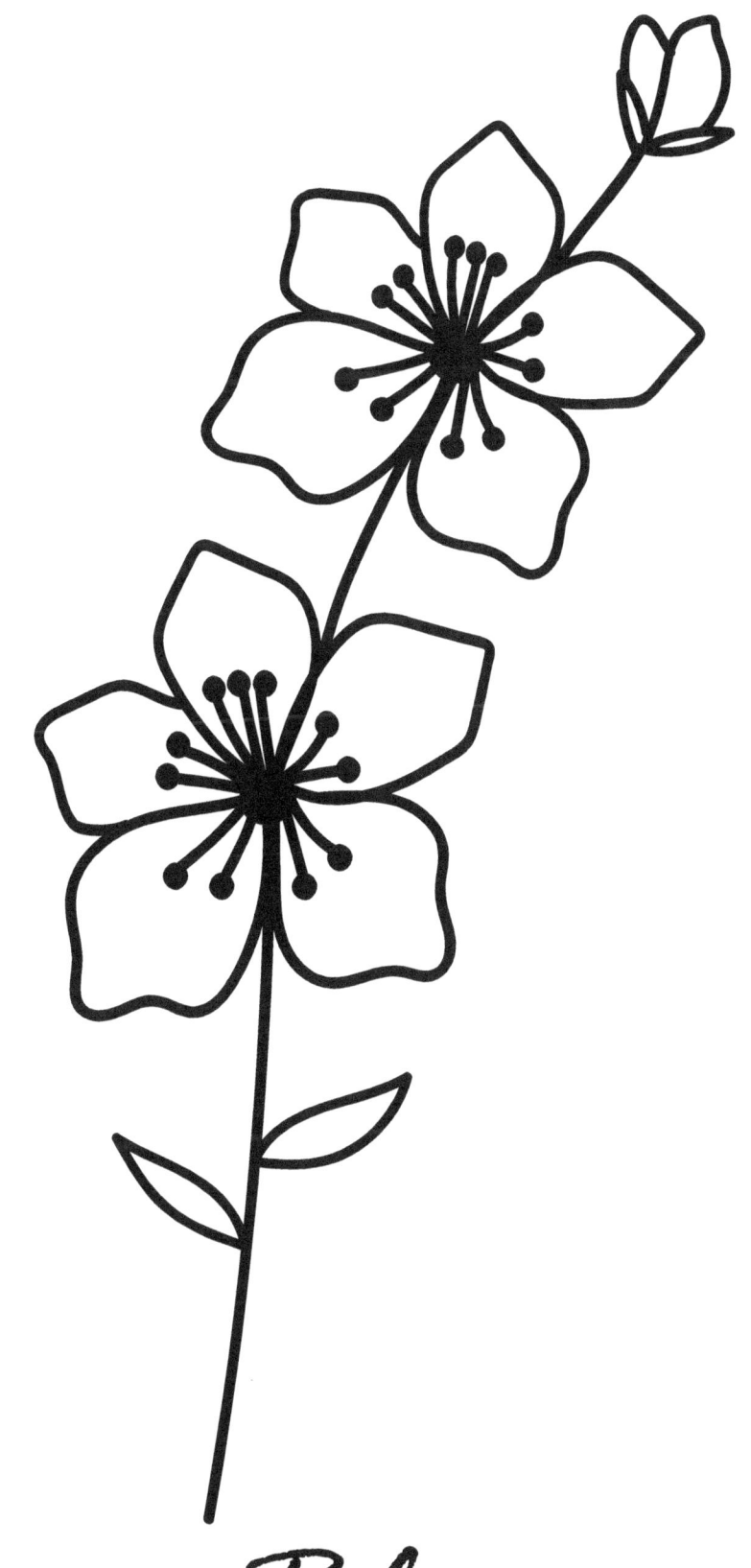

Cherry Blossom

This Page is Intentionally Left Blank to Prevent Bleed Through.

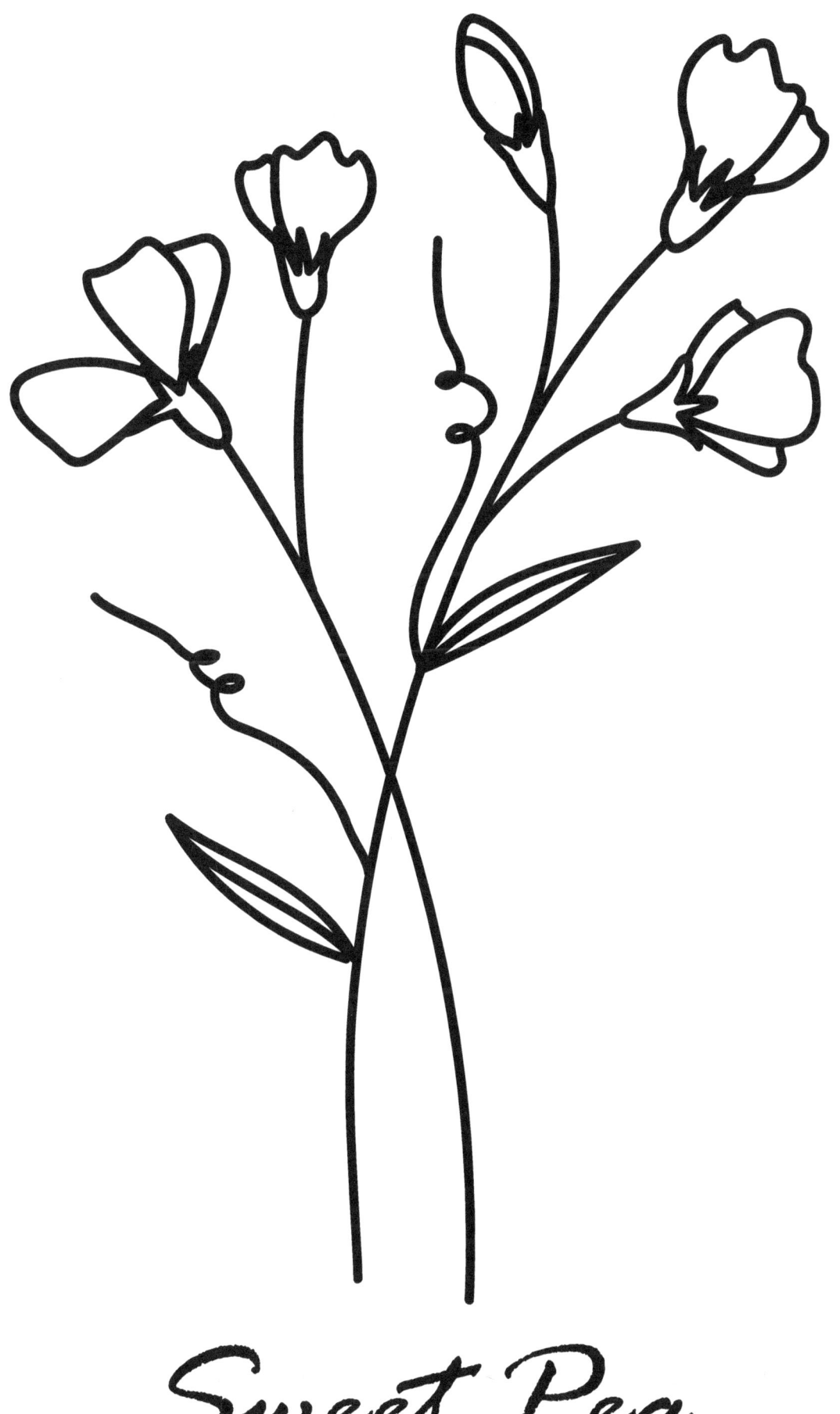

Sweet Pea

This Page is Intentionally Left Blank to Prevent Bleed Through.

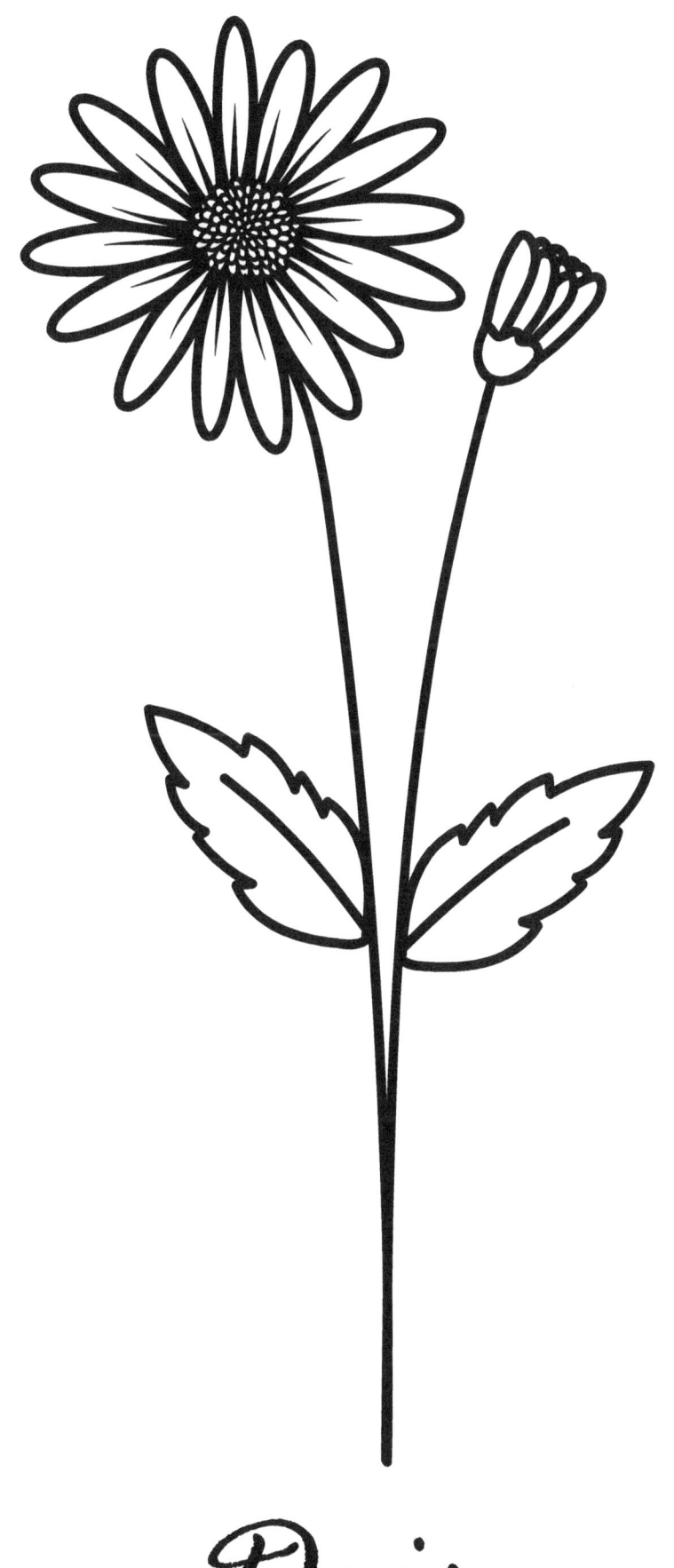

Daisy

This Page is Intentionally Left Blank to Prevent Bleed Through.

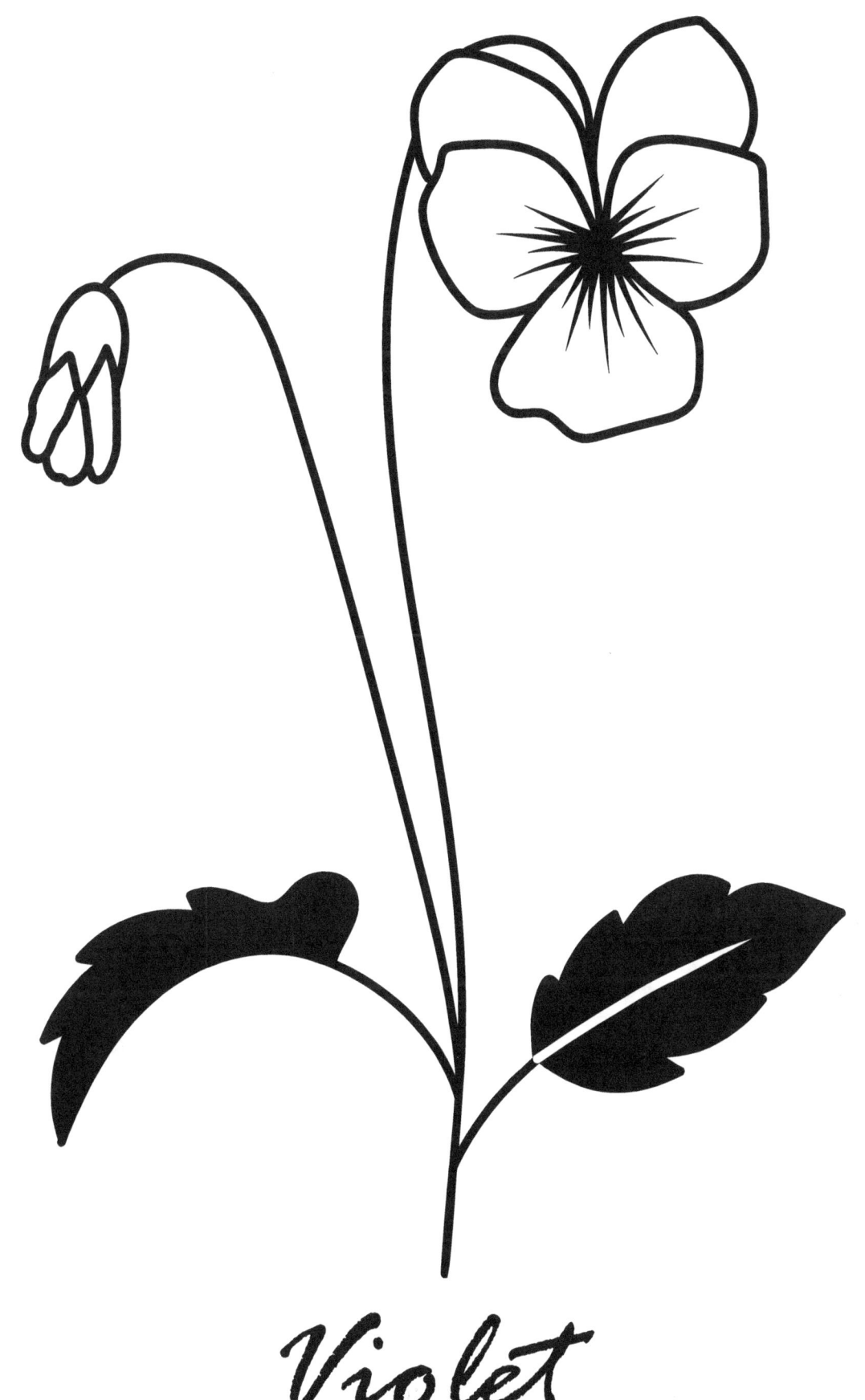

Violet

This Page is Intentionally Left Blank to Prevent Bleed Through.

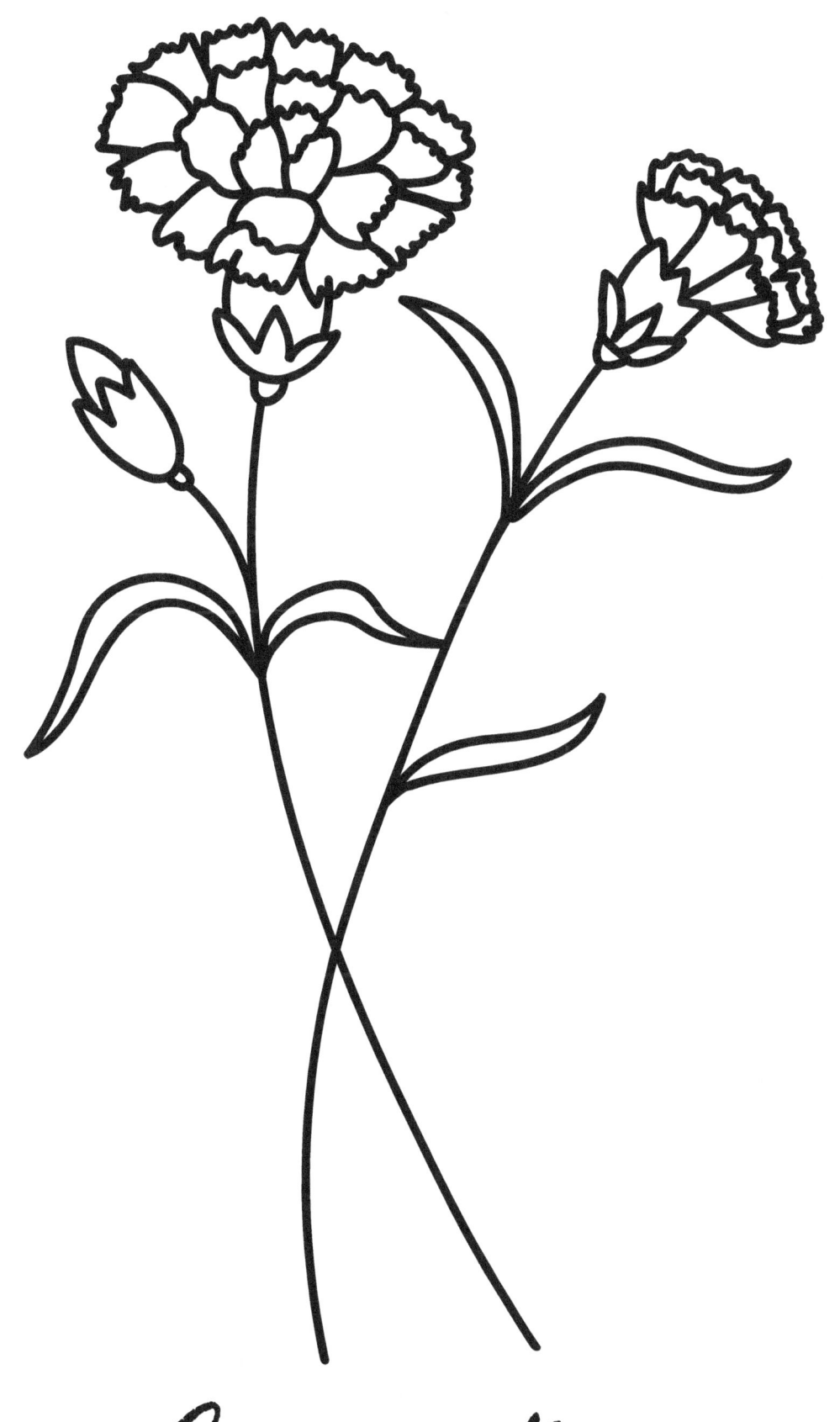

Carnation

This Page is Intentionally Left Blank to Prevent Bleed Through.

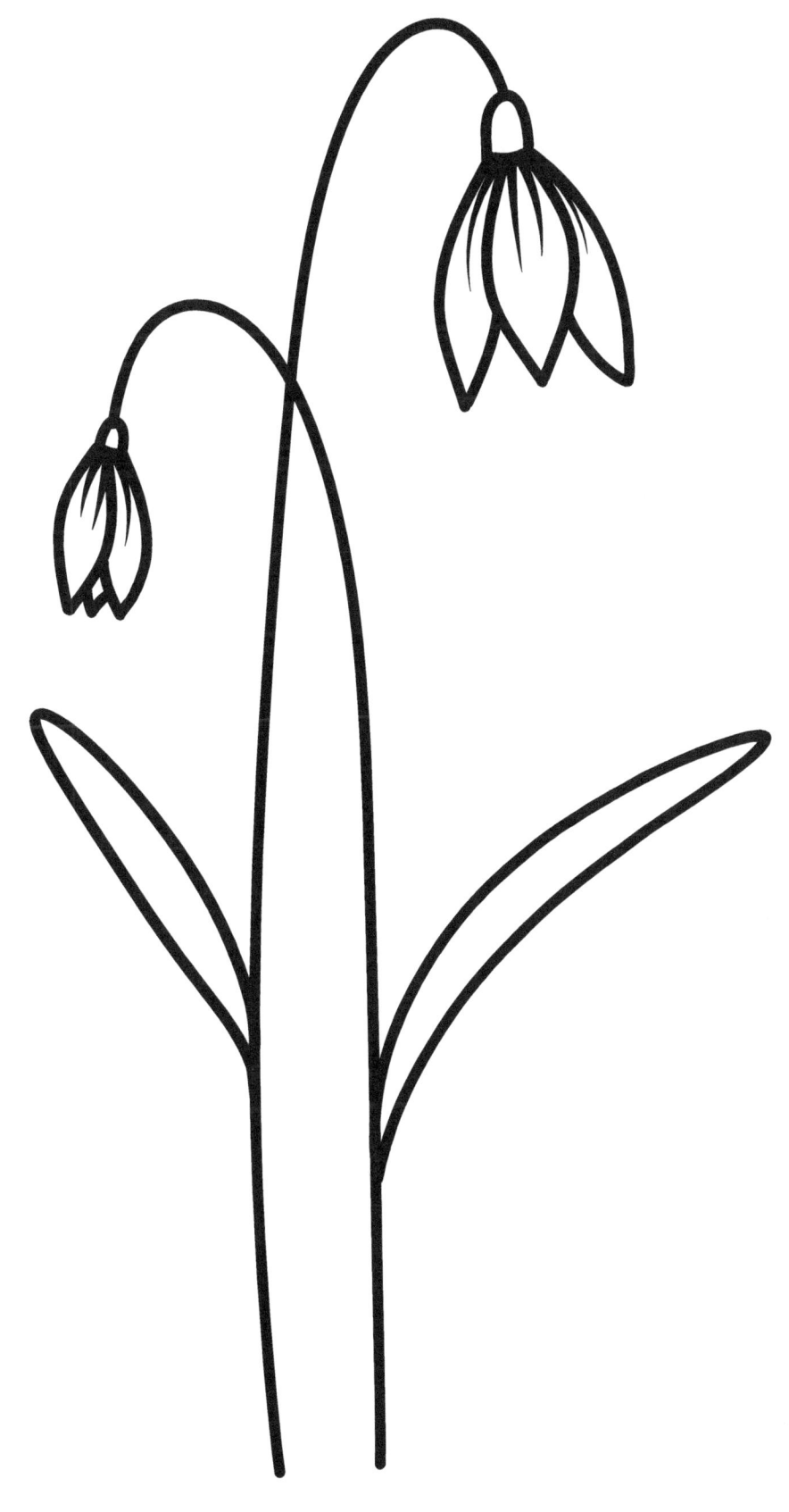

Snowdrop

This Page is Intentionally Left Blank to Prevent Bleed Through.

Identify and write the name of flower

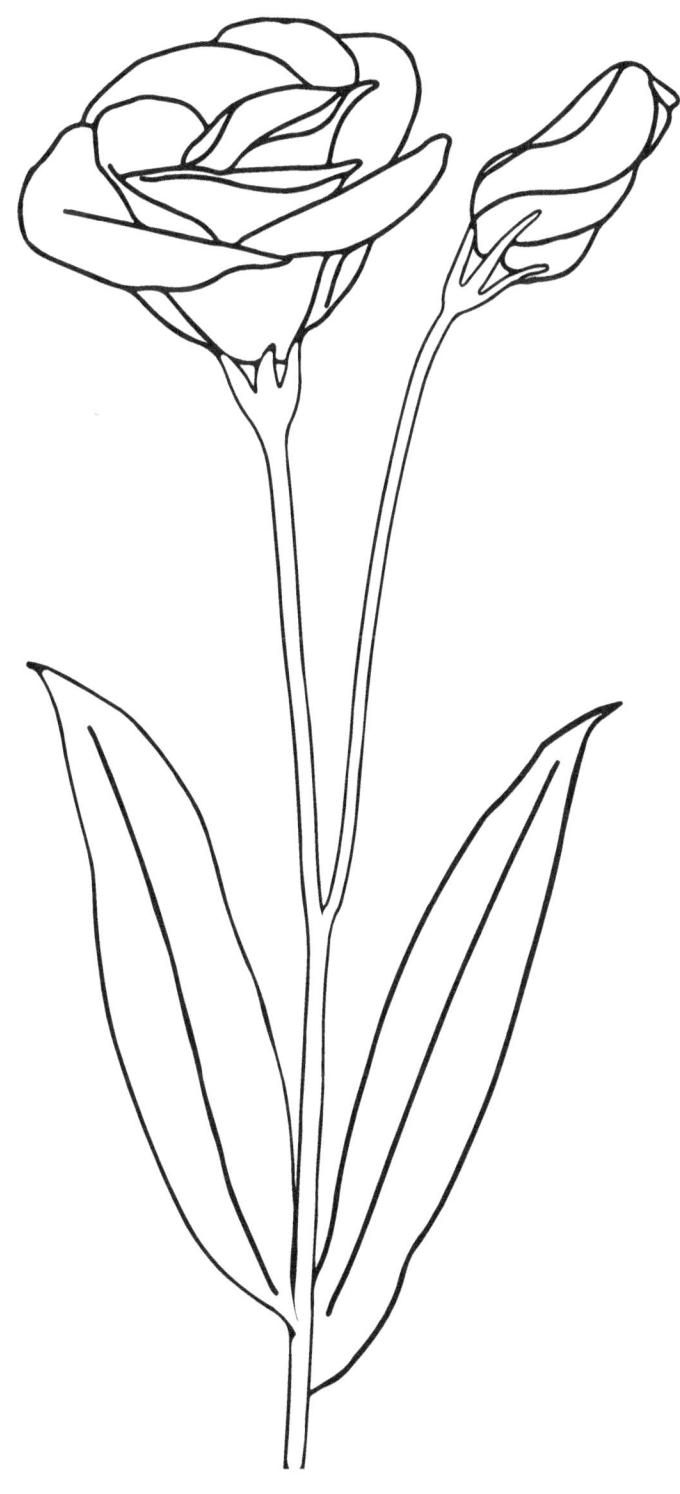

_____

This Page is Intentionally Left Blank to Prevent Bleed Through.

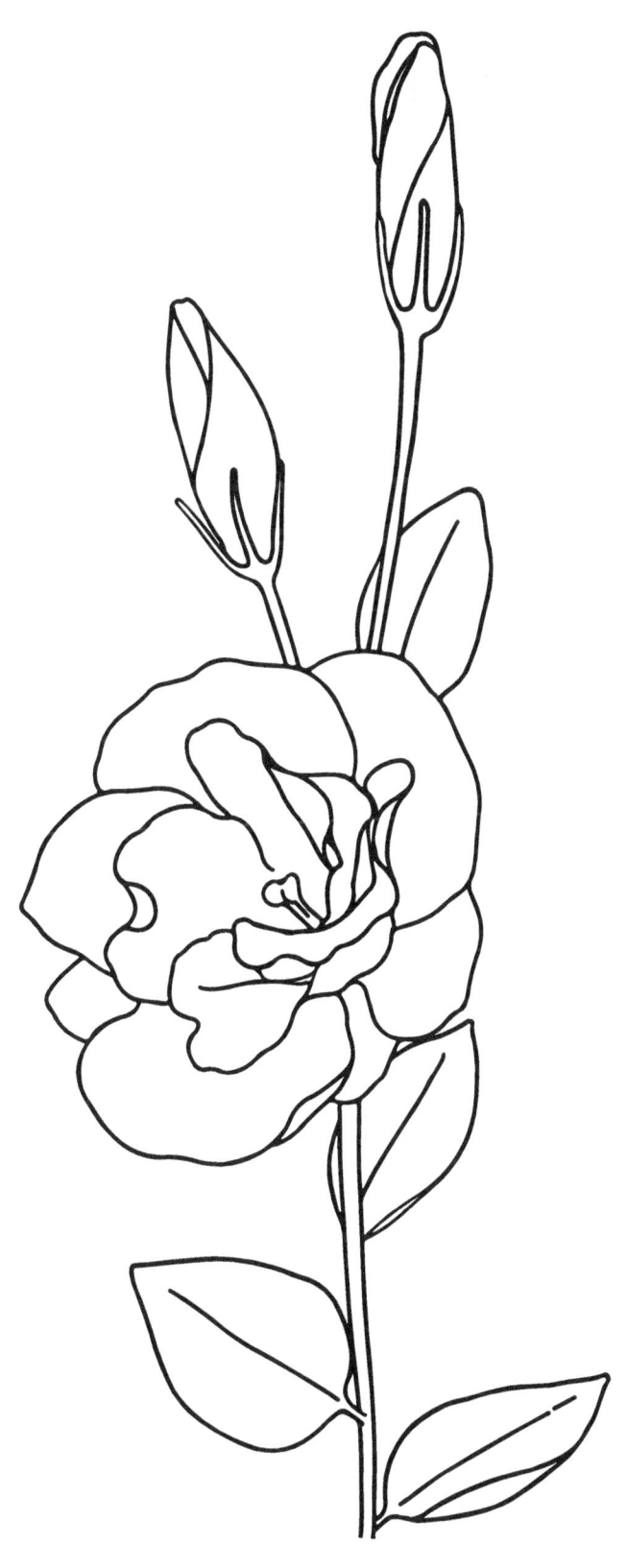

This Page is Intentionally Left Blank to Prevent Bleed Through.

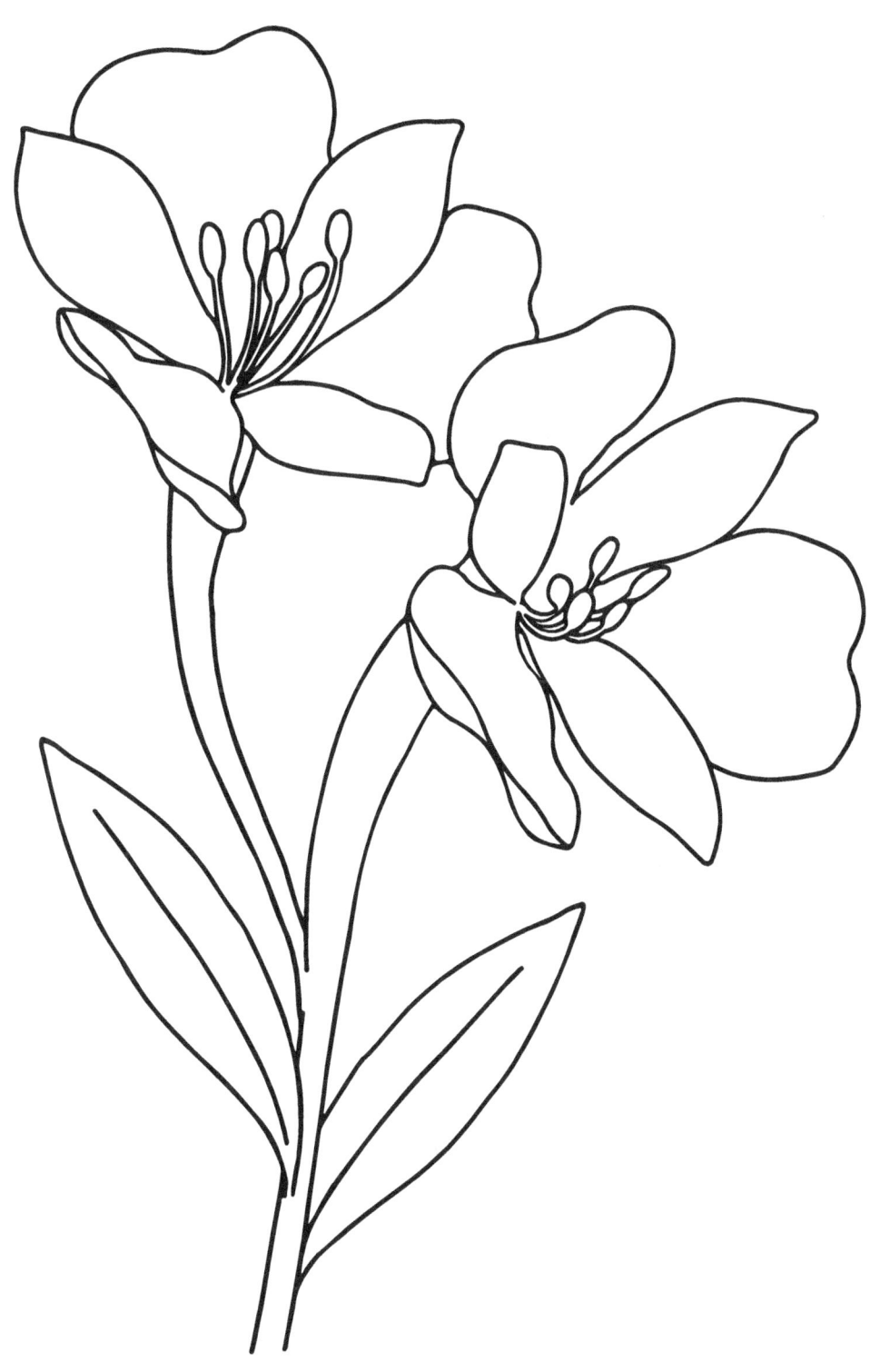

This Page is Intentionally Left Blank to Prevent Bleed Through.

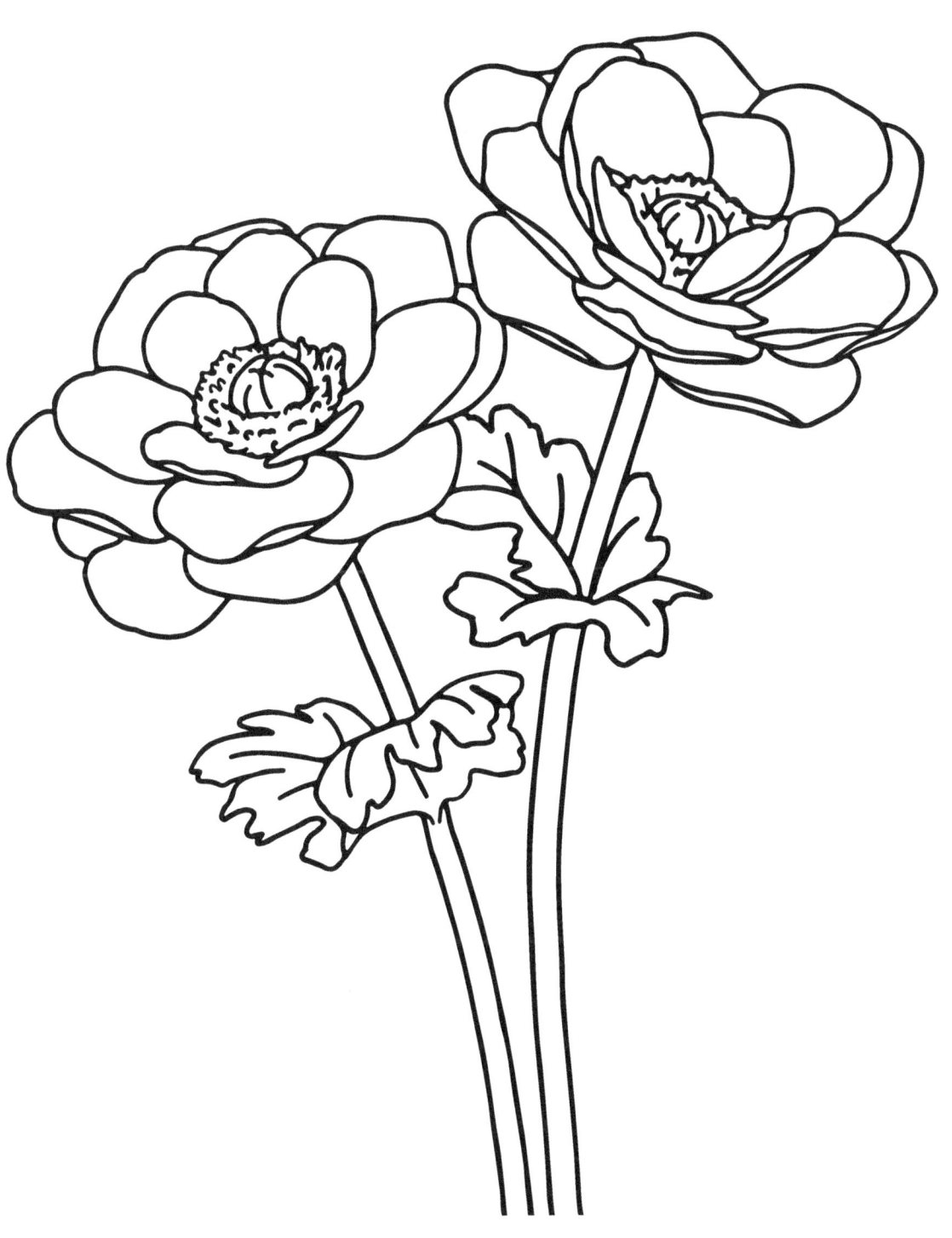

This Page is Intentionally Left Blank to Prevent Bleed Through.

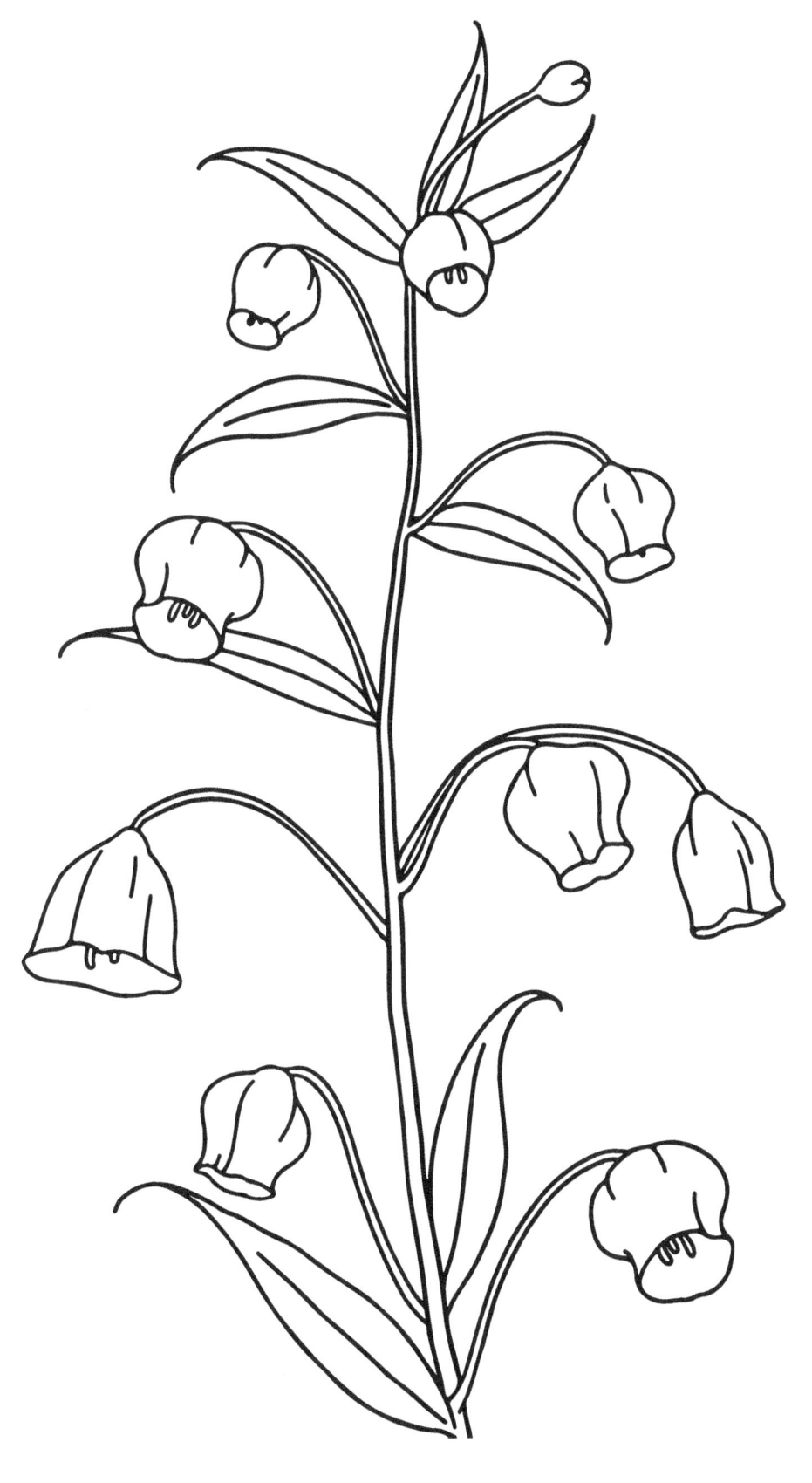

This Page is Intentionally Left Blank to Prevent Bleed Through.

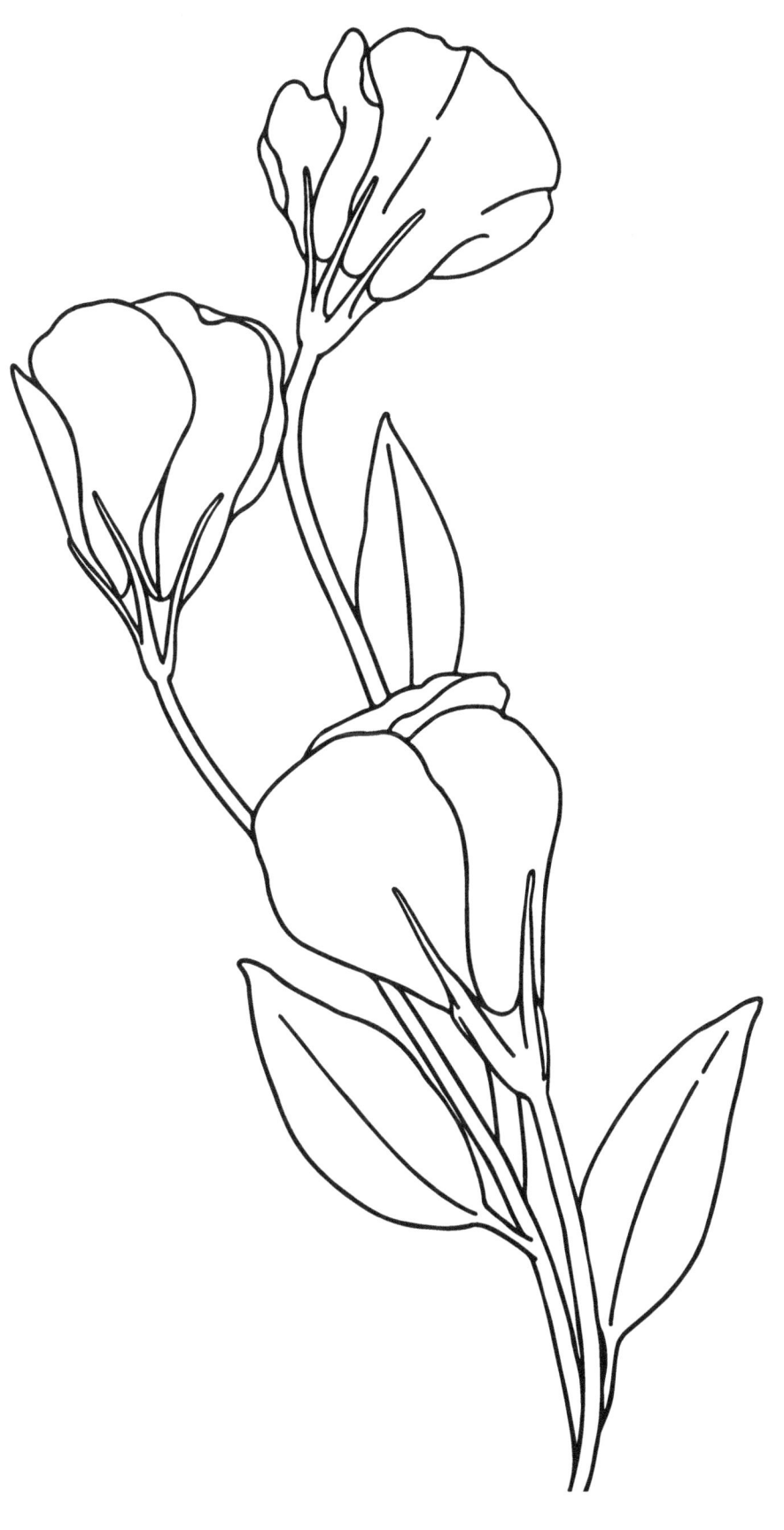

This Page is Intentionally Left Blank to Prevent Bleed Through.

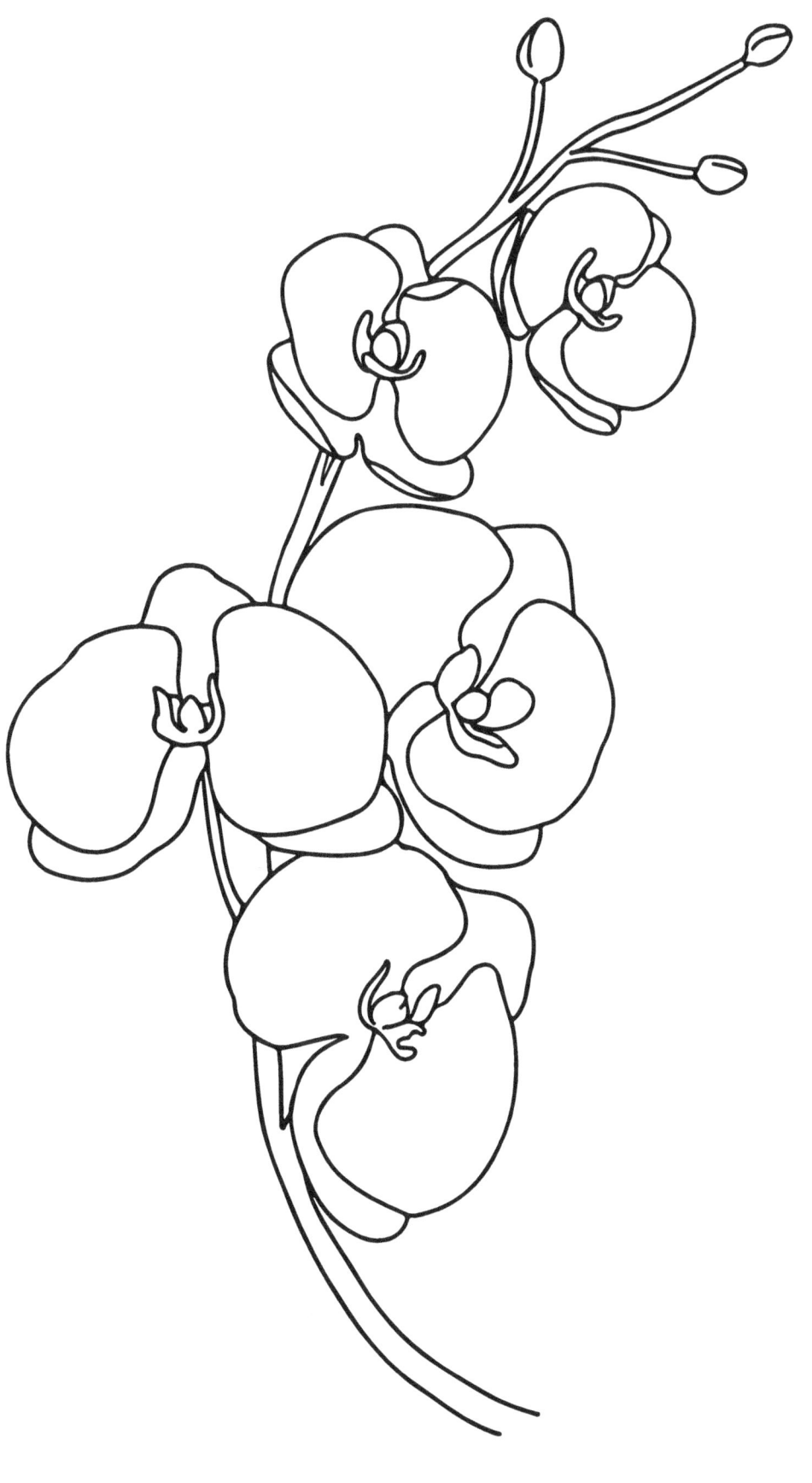

This Page is Intentionally Left Blank to Prevent Bleed Through.

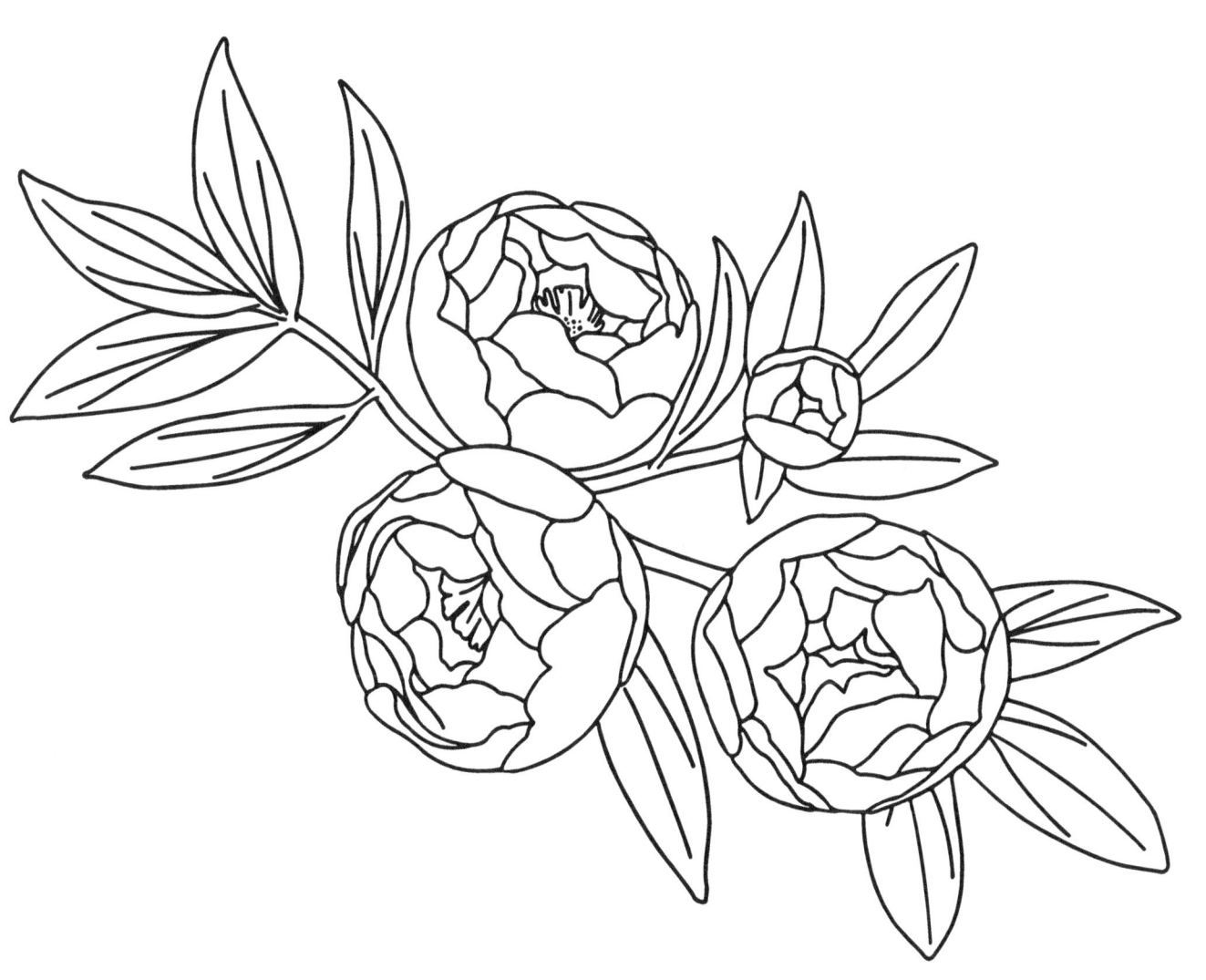

This Page is Intentionally Left Blank to Prevent Bleed Through.

www.ingramcontent.com/pod-product-compliance
Lightning Source LLC
Chambersburg PA
CBHW081002290526
45795CB00009B/3040